Contents

Preface 1

CORPORATE GOVERNANCE 3

CAPITAL BUDGETING 34

COST OF CAPITAL 52

LEVERAGE 75

WORKING CAPITAL MANAGEMENT 86

Preface

Make smart decisions and learn complete Corporate Finance in just one week. This book is written in simple and plain language to ensure that the students can grasp the concepts with great ease. As a university instructor for past 11 years I know how to make things easy.

This is my 7th book on investment. Previous books were highly appreciated and for that I am much obliged. Actually the succession of those books made me to take one step ahead and I wrote this book.

I am happy to launch this book with which you can cover and master your Corporate

Finance with great ease. Nevertheless this is most affordable and quality study material.

I am looking forward to come up with more books. Love you all the aspirants and may you succeed in your goals.

M. Imran Ahsan

<u>Ch.imranahsen@gmail.com</u>

Whats app# 00923465006818

CORPORATE GOVERNANCE

Corporate governance

In simple words corporate governance is a system by which a company is managed. This system includes the processes, techniques and rules to control, direct and operate the company.

Management of a company is a crucial part. There must be a strong system of corporate governance in place. A weak system can cause failure of the company.

Different practices of corporate governance exist in different organizations due to different geographical locations or due to different objectives of the firms. There are two theories which direct the corporate governance.

Shareholder theory: Under this theory the management team of the firm needs to work for common shareholders' wealth maximization. All the activities of the firm must be consistent with shareholders wealth maximization rule.

Stakeholder theory: This theory has broad spectrum. It states that the management team of a firm should work for all stakeholders (and not just common shareholders). The stakeholders of the firm can include shareholders, board directors, creditors, customers, suppliers, employees, regulatory bodies etc.

The current trends in corporate governance depict the mix of above two theories.

Stakeholder groups

**Company`s stakeholders:** A company`s stakeholders are all those who have interests in the company. Different stakeholders may or may not have conflict of interests. Following are main stakeholders of a firm;

Shareholders: Shareholders provide equity capital for the firm and hold residual claims of company`s assets after payment of all liabilities. Shareholders can be individuals or institutions who own at least one share in a company. Shareholders want the company to grow so their equity increases. They are also entitled for the dividends.

Shareholders have the voting rights to elect board of directors and for major other company`s decision making process. This board of directors is the representative of shareholders in the company. Board of directors manages all the affairs of the company through senior management and other staff. So, the shareholders have great power to influence the company matters. Some shareholders have major portion of shares and can influence the elections so they are collectively called controlling shareholders. Other than controlling shareholders there are minor shareholders who have little power to control or influence the company matters.

All the payments to shareholders are made at last stage in case of liquidity of the firm or dividend announcement. Before any shareholder gets paid all the obligations must be paid.

Creditors: These are the debt providers to the company in return for interest payment plus the principal amount. The creditors have no voting power so they cannot influence the company`s matters. They want that company must be generating enough cash flows from main business activities so they get paid according to the plan. Creditors are usually banks and bondholders of the firm.

Creditors hate if a company takes risks while the shareholders may want to take high risk with higher expected returns.

The creditors can restrict the activities of the firm by using covenants (These are the restrictions imposed by lender to borrower to protect lender's interests i.e. repayment of debt. Debt covenants reduce the default risk so it also reduces borrowing cost.).

Managers: Managers and other employees are the people who work for the company for remuneration. They want job security and maximum remuneration. Usually they get these two objectives when the company prospers. So they have interests like shareholders. Sometimes their interest conflict with the shareholders like firing a manger might be good for the company and shareholders but that's really bad for the employee.

Board of directors: Shareholders elect board of directors. They manage all the affairs of the company through hiring other employees (senior management). They are the representatives of the shareholders in the firm.

Customers: Customers are the buyers of goods or services of the firm. They want their company to produce high quality goods/services. They do not have any interest in the financial performance of the firm.

Regulatory bodies and government: The regulatory bodies want the company to work according to the law and protect the economy as a whole. The government wants the maximum tax revenues from the firm without hindering its operations. The government also has other interests like employment protection, no child labor, environmental affects etc.

Suppliers: These are the firms or individuals who supply the raw material to the firm. They are short term creditors so their interests are like creditors.

Principal-agent relationships and conflicts

Principal-agent relationship is formed when somebody (the principal) hires someone (the agent) to complete a task in interest of principal. If the interests of agent are different from principal, a conflict of interest is developed. For example if an employee is not working for the best interests of the shareholder.

Shareholders and manager/director conflict of interest: Directors are appointed by the shareholders to maximize the shareholders` equity. The directors may not take some risks which could maximize the equity but are too risky. The board directors are paid for their performance and if the company goes down by taking that risk, the board of directors could be blamed. So they usually avoid risk. In this case a conflict of interest arises.

The directors and managers usually have more access to latest information about company. This is called asymmetry of information.

The board of directors appoints managers. The managers want maximum remuneration and other perks. Their interests may also differ from shareholders in certain situations.

Controlling shareholders and minority shareholders: The controlling shareholders have majority of shares so they are highly influential in company matters. Controlling shareholder can exploit their control and take certain decisions which are not in best interest of minority shareholders.

Shareholders and creditors: The shareholders may want to reinvest the profits or borrow new funds to maximize their wealth but these two activities are not in best interests of creditors, because the creditors want a smooth flow of cash for debt repayment.

Customers and shareholders: Certain activities create conflict of interest between these two. For example increase in product price and reducing the quality of product or services.

Shareholders and suppliers: Like creditors the conflict of interests between these two could arise from same situations.

Shareholders and regulatory bodies: Company can adopt new policies which could defer tax payment or reduce tax payment. These activities are in best interest of shareholders but might conflict with regulatory bodies and government.

Stakeholder management mechanisms

Different stakeholders have different interests. These interests must be identified, and prioritized. Stakeholder management means maintaining good relationships with all the stakeholders. This can be done by effective engagement and communication.

The stakeholder management practices can be different from company to company and from country to country. However the basic guideline is to minimize any potential conflict of interest.

Stakeholder management components:
There are four components to manage relationships with stakeholders

Legal infrastructure: Legal infrastructure involves the rights and obligations of stakeholders defined by the law.

Contractual infrastructure: This includes the contractual agreement between all the shareholders. The companies generally have more control over contractual infrastructures.

Organizational infrastructure: It includes the company`s process, procedures and practices by which it manages the relationships with stakeholders.

Governmental infrastructure: The regulations imposed by the government and its regulatory bodies to manage rights and obligations of stakeholders.

Different mechanisms to manage stakeholder relationships are as follows;

Annual General Meeting (AGM): Annual general meetings are usually held after the completion of a financial year. The shareholders attend these meetings. They are presented the audited financial statements, the annual growth report and other documents by the management. The shareholders can ask questions about any concern if they have. Any individual who have the shares of a company can attend these meetings and vote. The shareholders who cannot attend the meeting can use proxy voting right. In *proxy voting* a shareholder can assign anybody to use his voting right.

Extraordinary general meetings can be called by the shareholders or management, whenever there is need for shareholders` approval to pass a resolution. The typical purposes of extraordinary meetings can include acquisitions, mergers, a material change in corporate governance of the company etc.

Resolutions can also by of two types; ordinary resolutions and special resolutions.

Ordinary resolution: These are of ordinary nature and may include appointment of auditor, board of director elections etc. A simple majority vote cast is required to pass an ordinary resolution.

Special resolution may include issues like acquisitions, mergers, a material change in corporate governance of the company etc. A two third or three fourth majority of all casted votes is required to pass special resolution.

Voting methods also vary. Simple voting means allocating total number of votes to elect a board member or to pass a resolution. In cumulative voting the total voting rights increases. Total voting rights in cumulative voting are equal to the number of votes held multiplied by number of board of directors. For example a shareholder having 100 shares and there are 5 members to be elected. Total 100 x 5 =500 votes can be casted by that shareholder. In this method a shareholder can cast all of his votes for the first member, and then can use all of his votes for second director and so on. In cumulative voting, minority shareholders enjoy a better representation in company matters.

In some cases the minority shareholders can have special privileges established by the law. These special situations include acquisitions and mergers. This is because these incidents can affect minority shareholders the most.

Company's board of directors and its committees

Board of directors is the representative of the shareholders in a company. It can monitor the management and its activities.

Composition of board of directors

There are two structures of board of directors "one-tier" and two-tier.

One- tier board of director: It is a single board. In one tier board of director structure there are two types of board members; Executive and non executive.

Executive: Also called internals. They are typically senior managers. They are employed by the company.

Non-executive: Also called externals. They are not employed by the company. These are the actual decision makers for the company.

Two-tier board: In two tier board there are two mutually independent boards; supervisory board and management board.

Supervisory board: It consists of non-executive members (externals).

Management board: It consists of executive members (internals).

For most of the companies it is mandatory to be qualified and experienced to be a board member. Each board member should be expert in one of the fields like finance, general management, strategic management, HR etc.

CEO duality: It means the CEO of a company also serves as chairperson of the board. This trend is changing and the CEOs and chairperson of the board are being separated.

Functions and responsibilities of the board:

The board of directors is the group of shareholders representative. The board is there to protect the shareholders` interests. They have two main duties; duty of care and duty of loyalty.

Duty of care: It means the board members are required to act on fully informed basis, in good faith and with due diligence

Duty of loyalty means they are required to act in best interest of shareholders.

In general board of directors has following functions and responsibilities;

- Hiring and firing of senior management according to the performance.
- Setting remunerations for senior management
- Setting of goals and objectives of the company
- Organization planning
- Make strategies to use company resources optimally
- Reviewing company`s performance
- Assuring the quality of financial statements
- Approval of capital structure

Remember the board of directors does not involve in day-to-day activities of the firm. For that purpose there is management team.

Board of directors committees: Typically board creates different committees and the board members are included in these committees according to their expertise. Some examples are;

Audit committee: It does the following functions;
- Recommend and appoint external auditors
- Setting auditor`s remuneration
- Monitor accounting policies and process
- Monitor and recommend internal and external control

Governance committee: Implement and monitor good governance practices.
It ensures that the practices are according to applicable law.

Remuneration committee: It recommends the amount and type of compensation that should be paid to directors and senior management.

Nomination committee: It nominates the qualified candidates for the board of directors. It makes sure that the nominated candidates fulfill the conditions imposed by corporate governance. This committee also oversees the nomination process, procedure and make sure that the board of directors is well balanced.

Risk committee: It determines the amount of risk the company is facing, risk tolerance of the firm and supervise the risk management team.

Investment committee: It assists the board in investment matters like acquisitions, mergers and expansions.

Factors that can affect stakeholder relationships and corporate governance

There are two types of factors which can affect stakeholders' relationships; Market factors and non-market factors.

Market factors include all the factors related to capital market. Non- market factors are all those factors which are not related to capital market. Market and non market factors can affect stakeholder relationships and corporate governance.

Market factors

Shareholder engagement: Shareholder engagement is the engagement of the company with shareholders through annual general meetings and analyst calls and other events like this.

Shareholder activism: It means all the activities adopted by the shareholders to create changes in the organization. The purpose of this activism is to create change so the company behaves in a certain manner. Remember that the shareholders want to maximize their equity.

Shareholder activism can include campaigns and lawsuit. Usually the law forbids the minority shareholders to sue board of directors.

Hedge funds face more shareholder activism as there is less transparency and less disclosure requirements by law.

Competition and takeovers: It include proxy fights (proxy fight means voting to a controlling group), tender offer (selling the shares to controlling group) and hostile takeover (an attempt of a company to acquire another company without the consent of management).

The shareholders usually analyze the financial statements and compare their performance with competitors. They tend to vote to hire or fire the senior management with respect to their performance.

Non-market factors

Legal environment: The legal environments in which the company exists and operates have crucial impact on stakeholders' interests and relationships. The countries under common law are considered best to protect the shareholder and creditor`s interests than all those countries which are under civil laws. Regardless of system the creditors are generally considered better protected than other stakeholders.

Media: Media is a crucial tool to change the general opinion. Lately the development and use of social media is being used to change the opinions of masses very quickly. The media can influence the reputation of a company and or its management or board members. The changed opinion can influence the stakeholder's relationships.

Corporate governance industry: Recently the demand for external corporate governance rating agencies has increased. The shareholders prefer the ratings provided by these agencies.

Drawbacks of poor corporate governance and stakeholder management and benefits of effective corporate governance and stakeholder management

Potential risks of poor corporate governance and stakeholder management:

- One stakeholder can gain extra advantage over the cost of other stakeholder.

- When the system is not well established the management can make poor decisions which are in their own favor are not for all stakeholders

- The legal and regulatory risks increases

- Company`s reputation is degraded
- The lower quality products will be produced and the demand will fall.

- The company with bad reputation struggles with new funds in times of need

- Te risk of default increases as the debt obligations would not be paid on time

Potential benefits of good corporate governance and stakeholder management:

- The default and legal risk can be reduced
- Good investment and other decision making
- Ability to raise low cost capital
- Increase in reputation
- No stakeholder can gain on the cost of others
- The company will be operating optimally so the cost of doing business falls. As a result profitability increases
- Good relations with customers will increase market demand
- The internal and external control will be effective

Analysis of corporate governance and stakeholder management

Analysts must consider following factors related to corporate governance and stakeholder management

Company ownership and voting: How the company is being owned and what is the voting structure in a company. Typically one share is considered a right of one vote. Some companies have different voting rights attached with different class of shares. For example in dual class structure, one class of shares has superior voting rights over other class of shares.

The superiority can be in form of more directors can be elected by one class and less number of directors can be elected by second class. Or one class has lower voting rights. Different classes of shares are issued to make sure that the pioneers or their hires have more control over the company.

A company who has more than one class of shares, trade at discount in the market.

Structure of board of directors: The analyst must look for the composition of the board members. The board must consist of balanced individuals with everyone should be expert in some field.

In addition to the expertise, the experience and reputation are also important. The members of a firm elected from within the organization, have better understanding of the firm. If more than one member is handing same matters, their potential conflict of interest should also be considered.

Remuneration and performance: Usually the remunerations information is available to the analysts. The remunerations are attached with the performance. These attached remunerations are based on short term and long term performances. These remunerations are cash salaries plus shares, options etc. The remunerations must be consistent with the company goals. If the remunerations are based on following terms it must raise a red flag.

- If the remunerations are only in cash and there is no equity offers.
- If the performance incentives are stable over time it may indicate that the goals were extremely easy to achieve
- If the remunerations are higher than comparable companies
- If the remunerations are based on company`s early years performance

Shareholders` composition: The analyst should also examine the composition of the shareholders. The shareholders can be large number of individual investors, one or small number of high net-worth investors, activist shareholders or other companies.

Small number of high net-worth investors can influence the company. The presence of activist shareholders can cause a sudden change in the management and its composition. The other institutions holding major portion of shares can provide better coordination between the companies but they will hinder any material change in the management.

**Strength of shareholder`s rights:** The analyst must consider whether the rights of shareholders' in a company are weak, average or strong in comparison with other companies. When the rights are strong the shareholders can change the company`s management by themselves. If they cannot, it means the rights are weak.

Long term risk management: The analyst should also consider how the company manages its long term risks to avoid failure.

ESG and investment analysis

ESG integration: While making investment decisions in companies, the investors consider these companies' impact on environment, society and governance. The _socially responsible and cautious investors_ avoid all those companies which are affecting negatively (to EGG). This practice is called ESG integration into portfolio planning and construction.

ESG can be divided into following sub-categories;

Environmental issues: Like increase in pollution, contaminating water etc.

Social issues: Like child labor, gender inequality etc.

Governance issues: Like bribery, corruption etc.

For example avoiding investment in tobacco companies is a common practice.

The investors set some criteria and eliminate all those companies from the list who are using 'bad practices' (causing social, environmental and governance issues). This can limit their investable asset and their overall returns might fall. The research on ESG and return suggests mixed results.

Implementation of ESGs in Investment

ESG integration can be implemented by following methods;

Negative screening: In this method we exclude some sectors or companies from our investment considerations. These excluded companies can involve in issues like increase in pollution, contaminating water, child labor, gender inequality bribery, corruption etc.

Positive screening: In this method we only include those companies who have good ESG related principles.

Relative or Best-in-class approach: In this method we only include those companies who have highest ESG score in the industry.

Thematic investment: In this approach we consider all those companies who are involved specific ESG goals like energy efficiency and climate change. For example companies using water and clean energy sources efficiently.

CAPITAL BUDGETING

Capital budgeting and its process

Capital budgeting: It is a process or method used by companies to evaluate capital projects. Capital budgeting helps in decision making of which project to choose and which project to leave, based on cost – benefit analysis.

Capital project means a project whose lifespan is more than one year.

Capital budgeting is very important and the finance manager should take good care in its process. Capital projects can include purchasing of costly machinery, installation of new plant etc.

Steps of capital budgeting process

1. **Idea generating:** Generating good ideas is the first and important step.
2. **Analyze individual proposals:** Gather maximum information about each idea. Evaluate and forecast the cash inflows and outflows and their timings and profitability.
3. **Plan capital budget:** Prioritize and organize all those projects who are within firm`s strategies.
4. **Assessing, monitoring and post auditing:** Examining how the project is performing, related to forecasts.

Typical capital budgeting projects include;

- **Replacement projects:** These projects can include replacing old machinery, plan and equipments, replacement of machinery etc.
- **Expansion projects:** Increase in size of the company.

- **New product:** Launching new products.
- **Regulatory projects:** The projects required by government or regulatory bodies.
- **Other projects:** like research and development projects whose cash flows are not certain.

Principles of capital budgeting.

Capital budgeting must follow following principles;

- **Decisions on capital budgeting are based on cash flows** and not only accounting concepts like net income. Moreover intangibles assets (patent rights, goodwill etc) are only considered when they cause a cash flow.
- **Timings of cash flows:** Timings of cash flows are very important. The managers should take good care to forecast the

timings of each cash flow. It is mainly because early inflows and delayed outflows are better than early out flows and delayed inflows due to time value of money.
- **Cash flows are based on opportunity costs:** Opportunity costs are those incomes which will be gone if we undertake a project.
- Cash flows should be considered **after deduction of taxes**
- **Financing cost is ignored** in capital budgeting because it is already being reflected in required rate of return (RRR or discount rate).
- **Cash flows are not considered as net income** because net income means revenues minus all costs, but here costs are not deducted from cash inflows.

Some basic concepts related to capital budgeting;

Sunk cost: It is the cost which is already made and cannot be recovered. Sometimes it is incurred before even starting a project like consultation cost.

Incremental cash flows: The cash flows if we have undertaken a project. Incremental cash flows = cash flows after the decision about a project have undertaken minus the cash flows before that decision.

Externalities: The effect of investment on other projects' cash flows of the same firm. When a new project decision has negative impact on another ongoing project it is called cannibalism. For example a company introduces a new car and existing customers of old model moves towards new car.
In capital budgeting, these externalities must be considered.

Conventional cash flows: It is the series of cash flows in which there is initial cash out flow and then there are cash inflows.

Unconventional cash flows: These cash flows do not follow the patterns of conventional cash flows. There might be initial inflow and then outflows. The direction of cash flows can change over time.

Mutually exclusive projects, project sequencing, and capital rationing

Mutually exclusive projects: These are the projects which compete with each other and only one project can be accepted. If two projects are mutually exclusive it means if we accept both projects, the one project will affect the cash flows of other project.

Independent projects are opposite to mutually exclusive projects. If two projects are independent of each other and are profitable the firm can choose both projects.

Project sequencing: It means the projects must be arranged in a manner so that investment on one project can create future investing opportunity in other project. If the first project gives us economic benefits the second project can be undertaken otherwise not.

Capital rationing: It means limiting the funds to a project. Capital rationing is done due to limited resources or due to availability of other more profitable projects. If the company has unlimited resources then it can invest in all the available projects and there is no need of capital rationing.

Net present value (NPV), internal rate of return (IRR), payback period, discounted payback period, and profitability index (PI)

Net present value: Net present value is the present value of all future cash flows minus initial investment.

The discount rate is the cost of capital adjusted for the risk.

Formula

NPV = Initial investment +

$$\frac{Cash\ flow1}{(1+r)^1} + \frac{Cash\ flow2}{(1+r)^2} + \ldots \frac{Cash\ flow'n}{(1+r)^n}$$

or

$$NPV = \sum_{t=0}^{n} \frac{CFt}{(1+r)^t}$$

Whereas;

"t" is the time of project or the point of time of each cash flow

CF is the cash flow (after tax)

"r" is the required rate of return or cost of capital.

With independent projects

The projects with NPV >0 can be accepted because this project will increase the shareholders wealth.

The projects with NPV <0 can be rejected because this project will decrease the shareholders wealth.

The projects with NPV 0 can be accepted or rejected because this project will not have any impact on shareholders wealth.

IRR: *IRR is the discount rate that makes the net present value of all the cash flows equal to zero.*

$$NPV = \frac{Cash\ flow1}{(1+irr)^1} + \frac{Cash\ flow2}{(1+irr)^2} + \ldots \frac{Cash\ flow\ n}{(1+irr)^n} = 0$$

Or

$$NPV = \sum_{t=0}^{n} \frac{CFt}{(1+irr)^t} = 0$$

Solve for "irr".

With independent projects
The projects with IRR >"r" can be accepted because this project will increase the shareholders wealth.

The projects with IRR <"r" can be rejected because this project will decrease the shareholders wealth.

The projects with IRR ="r" can be accepted or rejected because this project will not have any impact of shareholders wealth. It will generate the return just equal to cost of capital (cost of borrowing)

"r" is the cost of capital.

Limitations of NPV and IRR: These methods cannot be used when future cash flows are uncertain. These measures are also very sensitive to inflows and outflows of cash (timings and amount).

Payback period: It measures how much time it will take to return us original investment. We use the negative signs with outflows (and initial investment) and positive signs with inflows and take a sum until we reached at zero.

Example

year	0	1	2	3
Cash flow	-500	100	400	300
Cumulative cash flow	-500	400	0	300

As we see in this example the cumulative cash flows become zero in year 2, so the payback period is two years. In payback period the year 3 and following years are ignored.

If we have a project with following cash flows in which the payback is not a whole year then we use following formula;

year	0	1	2	3
Cash flow	-500	100	450	300
Cumulative cash flow	-500	400	50	350

Payback period=

Full years until recovery year +
$$\frac{un\text{-}recovered\, cost\ at\ the\ begining\ of\ recovered\ year}{Cash\ flow\ during\ recoverd\ year}$$

Payback period $= 1 + \frac{100}{450} = 1.223$ years

Discounted payback period: This method is same just like simple payback period but here we use discounted cash flows.

We first discount each cash flow with cost of capital and then add them up to get our payback period just like payback period.

A project with less payback period is better. The payback and discounted payback period methods measures the liquidity. But the decisions cannot be made solely on these two measures. These methods ignore the salvage value (sale value of the asset after its useful life) and the cash flows beyond the payback periods.

Profitability index: It is the present value of all future cash flows divided by initial investment.

$$PI = \frac{Present\ value\ of\ all\ cash\ flows}{Initial\ investment}$$ or

$$PI = 1 + \frac{NPV}{Initial\ investment}$$

PI<1 do not undertake the project

PI>1 undertake the project

NPV profile and comparison of the NPV and IRR methods

NPV profile: NPV profile means the graph of NPV and discount rate. It shows different NPVS at different discount rates.

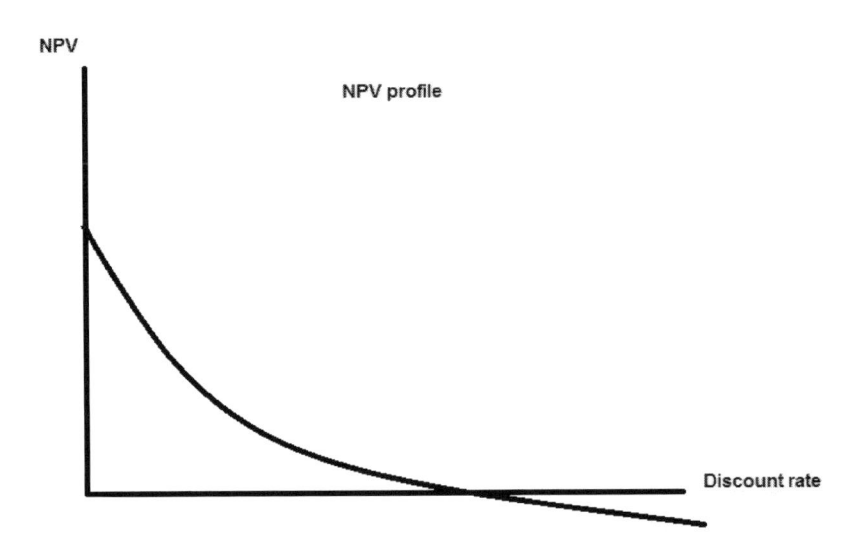

When the discount rate is zero the line hits the y-axis. When the NPV is zero the line hits X-axis.

The NPV and IRR both are good and produce same conclusions about two independent projects.

When the projects are mutually exclusive, both of these measures may take us to different ranking and conclusions. One project`s NPV might be greater than other but the IRR of other project might be greater than the project with higher NPV. In this case generally the NPV is preferred over IRR conclusions.

This difference in ranking may be result of
- Different timings of the cash flows between two projects
- Difference in sizes of two projects

We always go with the NPV method in case of conflict because the NPV implicitly assume that the inflows can be reinvested at existing discount rate (a reality based assumption). The assumption behind IRR is that we can reinvest at IRR. This is less realistic assumption because if the firm could reinvest at IRR then discount rate used in NPV should be equal to IRR.

If a project has multiple cash inflows and out flows, its IRR could be zero or multiple IRRs. In this case the IRR method fails. This type of project can still be profitable. In this case as we have already mentioned we prefer the NPV conclusion.

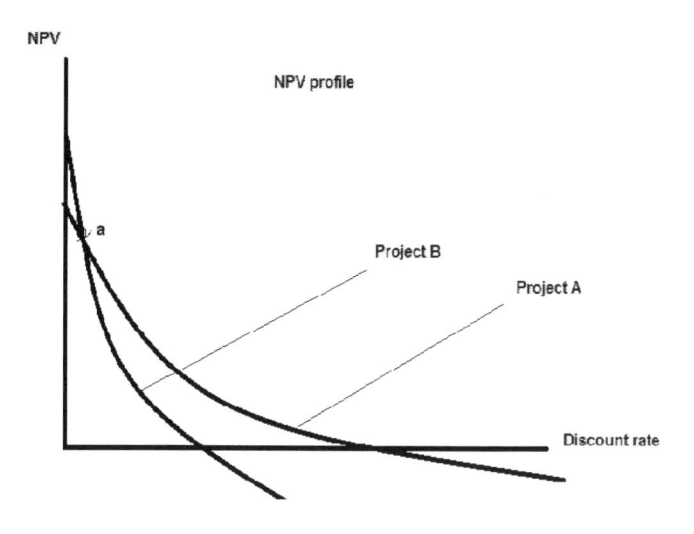

Sometimes we come up with same NPV of two projects at a specific discount rate as shown in above graph. At point "a" the NPV of both projects is same (the point is called crossover). This happens due to difference in timings of cash flows. Surely the project A has better NPV at most of the discount rate. If your discount rate is higher than point a`s discount rate then the project A is better.

Comparison of NPV and IRR: The NPV is preferred over IRR because it is more reliable in case of zero or multiple IRR. But the NPV does not consider the size of the project. A project of 100 million with NPV of $500 might not be as good as another project of 50 million with NPV of $500.

The IRR method however, gives us the per dollar return. But the IRR can be zero or there can be more than IRR.

Relations between NPV and share price

The NPV of a project is calculated by the project managers of the firm while the share price and company value mostly depend on the collective expectations of the investors in the market.

Theoretically speaking, positive NPV of different projects announced by the company should signal the market to increase the share price proportionately. But this does not happen usually, because of differences in the expectations of the managers and investors.

If the investors think that the new project will add more value to the firm than the what have been forecasted by financial managers, they will drag the share price (and value of company) even more than proportionate and vice versa.

COST OF CAPITAL

Weighted average cost of capital (WACC)

Weighted average cost of capital is the cost to raise capital. Companies have different types of funds for its capital need. They can borrow from banks and from investors (bonds) by issuing preferred stock and issuing common equity. The weighted average cost of capital is the aggregate cost of all these types of funds.

WACC= $W_d*K_d(1-t) + W_{ps}*K_{ps} + W_{ce}*K_{ce}$

Whereas

W_d means proportionate weight of debt in the total funds

K_d is the rate of interest to be paid to the lenders. It can be the yield to maturity of existing debt.

W_{ps} is the weight of preferred stocks in total funds

K_{ps} is the cost of preferred stocks which investors are required to invest in preferred stock.

W_{ce} is the weight of common equity

K_{ce} is the cost of common equity which investors are required to invest in the firm. This the most difficult one to calculate

Usually the debt is tax deductible so we have used (1-t) with K_d.
That means after tax cost of debt.

So the WACC is nothing but a weighted mean.

The WACC is the rate at which a company can raise funds. So this is also the discount rate at which capital budgeting should be calculated on. If IRR is greater than WACC then the project is viable otherwise not.

WACC is also opportunity cost for the company. Imagine if the company has not raised these funds to finance certain assets, it could have saved this cost.

Effect of taxes on cost of capital

Generally the debt is tax deductible so the companies and investors are interested in after tax cost of debt. That why we have use $Kd(1-t)$ in WACC. The cost of preferred stock and common equity are not tax deductible. The payments to common equity holders and preferred stock holders have no impact on WACC in terms of tax.

Determination of targeted capital structure and WACC

The weighted average cost of capital can be explicitly disclosed by the management. This explicitly disclosed weight is the targeted capital structure for the firm. If the targeted capital structure is not explicitly disclosed then an analyst can use the current weight of capital structure as targeted capital structure.

Another way to determine targeted capital structure is the use of industry average. If there is a particular trend in capital structure, for example the decreasing weight of debt and increasing weight of preferred stocks, this trend can be used in estimation of targeted capital structure.

Always remember to use the current market value of capital structure while quantifying the capital.

Marginal cost of capital, investment opportunity schedule and optimal capital budget

Marginal cost of capital (MCC) is the additional cost which the firm will bear while raising additional units of capital. For example, if the firm can raise debt capital at 10% the marginal cost of debt capital is 10%.

MCC has increasing trend because when the firm raise more and more capital additional cost increases.

On the other hand when firm involves in launching more and more investment projects, then the every new project usually gives less and less return (IRR). It is mainly because at first, the firm tries to invest in a project with highest IRR and then second project with second highest IRR and so on. So the investment opportunity schedule line has negative trend.

Then how much capital a firm should raise and invest? As long as the IRR is greater than cost of capital the firm is adding value in shareholders` equity.

We can understand this with the help of following graph;

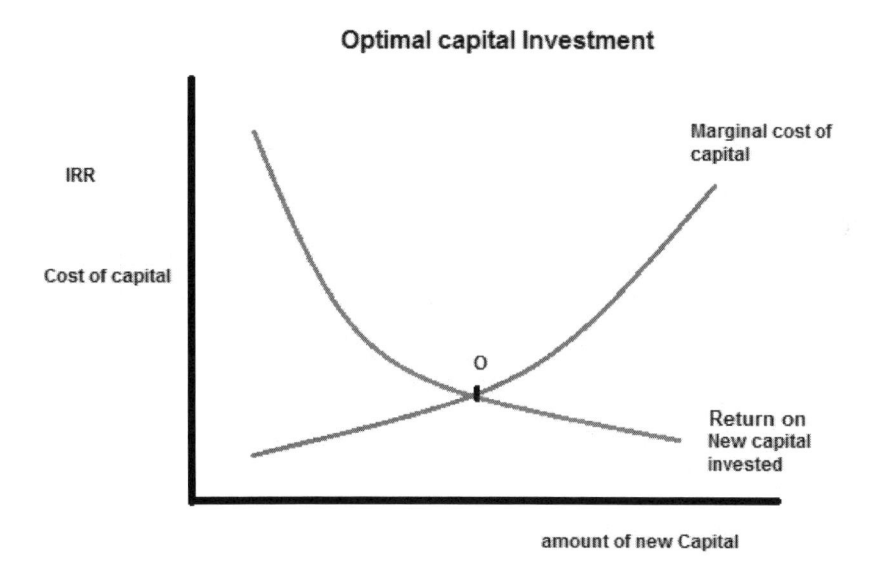

Optimal capital Investment

IRR

Cost of capital

Marginal cost of capital

O

Return on New capital invested

amount of new Capital

From lower level to Up to point "O" MCC is lower than IRR, the firm is adding value to the shareholders` equity. After the point "O" the MCC is higher than IRR so the firm should stop at point "O" and must not raise further capital. The point "O" is the optimal level when the MCC line intersects the marginal return on that fund (IRR).

Role of MCC in determining the NPV

The net present value is the present values of all future cash flows minus original investment. To calculate present value we discount the future cash flows at an appropriate discount rate usually the WACC.

By using WACC as discount rate we assume that

- The total risk of the firm will remain same during the life of project and
- The risk of new project is same as the firm's total risk

But in reality risk of a project may differ from the firm's total risk so we should make some adjustments in discount rate while calculating NPV.

If a project is more risky (than firm's total risk profile), then the discount rate should be higher than WACC
If a project is less risky (than firm's total risk profile), we should use lower discount rate than WACC.

Cost of debt capital using the yield-to-maturity approach and the debt-rating approach

The debt is generally tax deductable so we use Kd(1-t) in WACC to calculate after tax cost of debt. This debt can be a bank loan or the bonds issued by the company.

If the debt is not tax deductible the only Kd would be the cost of debt.

Following are two methods used to estimate a firm`s pretax cost of debt;

YTM approach
Debt-rating approach

YTM approach: It is the total return on a bond if it is held until maturity. The YTM equates the present value of coupon and principal payments to the current market value of the bond.

$$P0 = \sum_{t=1}^{n} \frac{C_t}{(1+YTM)^t} + \frac{FV}{(1+YTM)^n}$$

Whereas

P0 is the current market price of the bond

"t" is the time period

Ct is the coupon payment in period t

FV is the face value

YTM is the yield to maturity

For example;

A Bond with 4years of maturity and coupon rate of 5.5% at price of 102 the YTM can be calculated with the help of calculator as follows

n=4, PV=-102, PMT=5.5, FV=100, calculate 1/y

Debt rating approach: If the firm`s debt is not being traded in market or the market is very illiquid, we can use debt rating approach to calculate pretax cost of debt by using other debt issued by the same company with same maturity. If it is also not available then we can estimate it by using a comparable company`s comparable debt of same maturity. The comparable debt and company can have following characteristics

Same sized company

Same industry

Same business

Same risk exposure

Debt with similar risks etc

Cost of non-callable, nonconvertible preferred stock

Non-callable preferred stock is the preferred stock which cannot be redeemed by the issuer. Non-convertible preferred stock is the preferred stock which cannot be converted into common stocks by the investor.

The holder of preferred stock does not have any voting right.

The cost of preferred stock can be calculated as;

$$K_{ps} = D_{ps}/P_{ps}$$

Whereas

K_{ps} is the cost of preferred stock

D_{ps} is the dividend on preferred stock

P_{ps} is the market of preferred stock

Remember that the cost of preferred stock is non-tax deductible.

Measurement of cost of equity capital

Cost of equity is the minimum rate of return a firm should offer to investors to purchase its shares in primary market. Usually cost of equity is calculated using CAPM and dividend discount models and occasionally using Bond-yield plus risk-premium approach.

Cost of equity using CAPM model

Cost of equity using CAPM model = $E(R_i) = R_f + \beta_i[E(R_m) - R_f]$

$E(R_i)$ = expected rate of return on "i" security which is cost of equity to issuer.

R_f = Risk free rate of return

$E(R_m)$ expected market rate of return

B_i = Beta of investment. It is the systematic risk measure.

Cost of equity using Dividend discount model:

Dividend discount model consider the current market price and expected future dividends of a security. The rate which equates all future dividends to its current market price is the cost of equity (also called required rate of return).

As RRR and share price are inversely related. An increase in RRR would reduce the share price and vice versa. It can also be explained in another way. A reduction in the price of equity will increase expected return.

If the dividends are growing at a constant rate we can use Gordon's constant growth model to calculate cost of equity;

$P_o = D_1/(K_{ce} - g)$
And solve for K_{ce}

Whereas P_o is the current price of the common stock
D_1 is the next dividend
K_{ce} is the cost of common equity
"g" is the growth rate of dividend

K_{ce} is also called required rate of return by investors.

The growth rate g= b x (return on equity)

'b'= earnings retention rate or (1- dividend payout rate)

Bond-yield plus risk-premium approach:
According to this approach the cost of equity must be cost of bond plus risk premium for the common equity.

K_{ce} = K_d + risk premium

Beta and cost of capital for a project (PURE PLAY method)

In CAPM model we use beta for systematic risk of a security in comparison to market risk.

Cost of capital using CAPM model = $E(R_i) = R_f + \beta_i[E(R_m) - R_f]$

For a publically traded company the calculation of beta and cost of equity is easy.

But if the company is not being traded in the market or there is no active market for that company is available then we use a method called PURE PLAY to estimate beta.

Following steps can be followed to estimate beta for PURE play method;

1. Select a comparable company. The comparable company is the one who has similar capital structure, undertaken similar projects and similar types of risk facing company.
2. Calculate the beta of that company.
3. Unlever the beta of comparable company by removing the effect of financial leverage. Following formula can be used in unlevered process

$$\beta Asset(c) = \beta equity[+ \frac{1}{1 + (1 - tc)\frac{Dc}{Ec}}]$$

Whereas

$\beta Asset(c)$ is the unlevered beta of comparable company

$\beta equity$ is the equity beta of comparable company which we have estimated in second step

"tc" is the marginal tax rate of comparable company

Dc is the total debt of comparable company

Ec is the total equity of the comparable company

4. Now we have to lever this beta to adjust it to come up with the beta of out project.

$$\beta project = \beta asset(c)[1 + (1 - tc)\frac{Dc}{Ec}]$$

Whereas "tc" is the marginal tax rate of comparable company

Dc is the total debt of comparable company

Ec is the total equity of comparable company

Country risk premiums and cost of equity

The use of CAPM to estimate cost of equity is tricky in underdeveloped and developing countries because the beta does not capture country risk. A country risk premium is added in market risk to come up with a better estimate of cost of equity.

How to estimate country risk premium:
Following formula can be used to estimate country risk.

$$CRP = \text{Sovereign yield spread} \times \frac{\text{Annualized SD of equity index in developing country}}{\text{Annualized SD of sovereign bond market in terms of developed market currency}}$$

Whereas

CRP is the country risk premium

Sovereign yield spread = Developing country`s government bond yield denominated in *developed country currency − Treasury bond yield on a similar maturity bond in a developed country*

SD is standard deviation

After adding CRP the CAPM would be like this

Cost of equity using CAPM model =
$E(R_i) = R_f + \beta_i[E(R_m) - R_f + CRP]$

Marginal cost of capital schedule and breakpoints

Marginal cost of capital is the cost of raising additional units of capital. It tends to increase as the firm raise more and more capital. The firm can raise capital by, issuing debt (bonds), by shares (equity) or preferred stocks.
The one component of capital can affect other component of capital. If a firm raise more debt capital the cost of equity also increases

because the firm is getting more risky and the investors want higher required rate of return to invest in equity capital. Cost of capital also has uptrend because of debt covenants (the restrictions imposed by lenders on the borrower.

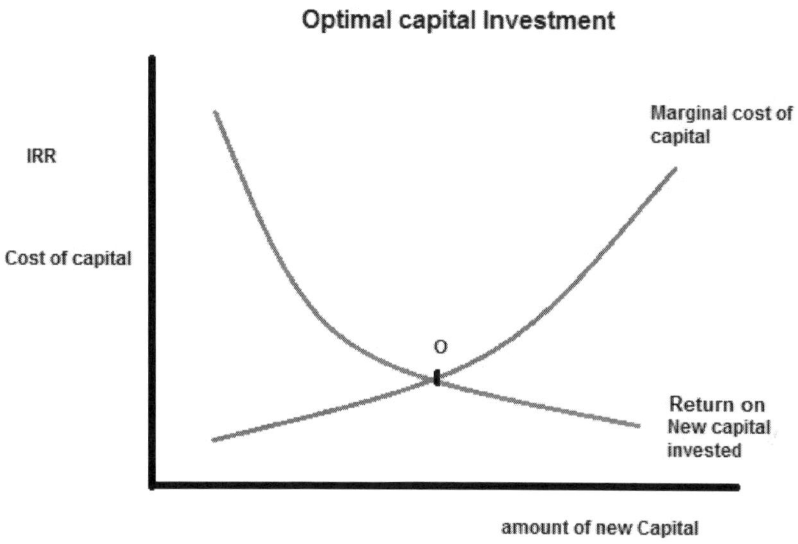
Optimal capital Investment
IRR
Cost of capital
Marginal cost of capital
O
Return on New capital invested
amount of new Capital

Breakpoint: Whenever any component of WACC changes which changes the WACC, break point occurs. In reality, the MCC is not a smooth upward graph, but is a step up graphs and every start of the step is called break point as flowing graph shows;

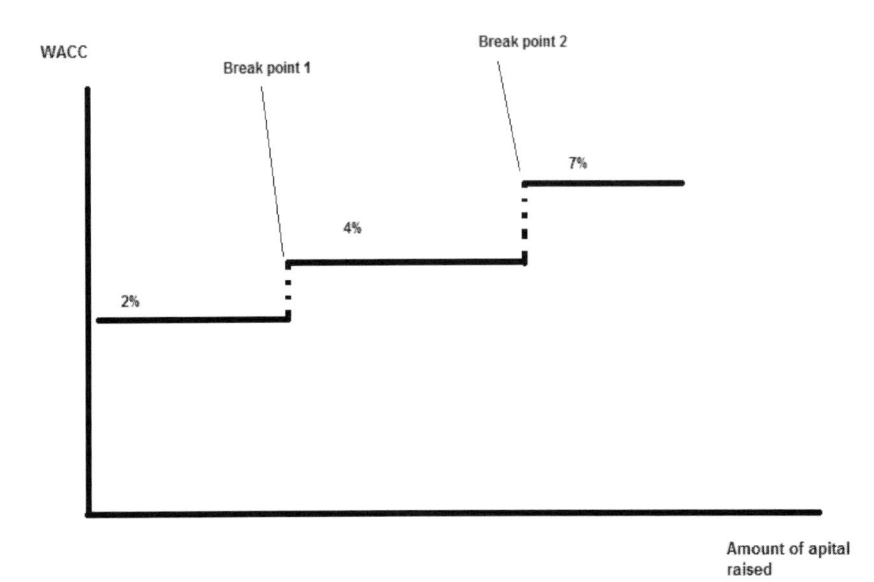

WACC

Break point 1

Break point 2

2%

4%

7%

Amount of apital raised

Formula to calculate break point;

Break point = amount of capital at which one component`s cost of capital changes/weight of that component in new capital structure

Break point is the amount of capital at which the cost of capital changes.

Flotation costs

Flotation cost: Companies have to bear some cost in the process of raising additional capital. These costs are called flotation costs. The amount of flotation cost depends on the amount of and types of capital being raised.

For example the flotation cost in case of debt and preferred equity is negligible. In case of common equity, the flotation cost could be very high (usually 2% to 7% of capital being raised). Usually a major portion of flotation cost comprise of investment bank`s fee (the investment bank who helps the company to raise capital).

Correct treatment of flotation cost: As the floating cost is one time outflow, it should be added into first time outflow of the project. Suppose a project has initial outflow of $5million and the project was totally financed by equity capital. The flotation cost is 2% of equity capital. The first outflow of the project should be

$5m + (5 million x 2%) = 5000000+100000= $5100000

And this initial investment is used as outflow with negative sign.

Incorrect treatment of flotation cost:

Some argues that the flotation cost is incurred during raising equity capital so it should be added in cost of equity. In this case the WACC increases and later while evaluating the project we would be discounting the project at higher discount rate. With this treatment we will come up with wrong estimates of NPV of the project.

LEVERAGE

Leverage, business risk, sales risk, operating risk, and financial risk

Leverage: Leverage usually means use of debt in a company`s cost structure. Here leverage means use of fixed cost.

Leverage can be of two types; operating leverage (depreciation and rent etc) and financial leverage (use of borrowed money and paying fixed interest).

Analysis of leverage is important because highly leveraged company`s profits and losses can be magnified. Moreover highly leveraged company`s risk characteristics also increases.

Business risk: Risk means uncertainty about the future (of the firm). Business risk of a firm consists of sales risk and operating risk.

Sales risk: It is the uncertainty of sales in future.

Operating risk: It arises from operating leverage. If a company has greater proportion of fixed operating cost relative to variable cost, the firm has greater operating risk.

Financial risk: It arises from the financial leverage. If a company has more debt (so it has to pay fixed interest rate) relative to common equity in capital structure, more the financial risk the company has.

Degree of operating leverage, the degree of financial leverage, and the degree of total leverage

Degree of operating leverage: It is the percentage change in operating income due to percentage change in sales. It measures the sensitivity of EBIT towards sales. It can also be defined as "measurement of firm`s operating risk".

Formula;

DOL = % change in operating income/% change in sales

$$DOL = \frac{\%\Delta\ EBIT}{\%\Delta\ in\ sales}$$

$$DOL = \frac{(sales - variable\ cost) \div sales}{(Sales - variable\ cost - fixed\ operating\ cost) \div sales}$$

$$DOL = \frac{PQ - VQ}{PQ - VQ - F}$$

Whereas

P is the per unit price of sales

Q is the total quantity of sales

V is the per unit variable cost

F is the total fixed operating cost

PQ is the total value of sale

VQ is total variable cost

The above formula can also be used to calculate DOL at any level of sales.

Interpretation: Let's say we come up with a DOL of 3%. What does it mean? It means if the sales changes (increase or decrease) by 1% then, our operating income will change by 3%.

More the company has fixed cost in total operating cost, more the company is facing operating risk and higher the degree of operating leverage.
Moreover the DOL also inversely related to sales, and variable cost.

Degree of financial leverage (DFL): It is used to measure the financial risk. DFL is the percentage change in net income due to percentage change in operating income. So, it measures the sensitivity of net income towards operating income.

$$\text{DFL} = \frac{\%\Delta \text{ net income}}{\%\Delta \text{ EBIT}}$$

Or

$$\text{DFL} = \frac{\text{Sales} - \text{variable cost} - \text{Fixed cost}}{\text{Sales} - \text{variable cost} - \text{fixed operating cost} - \text{interest expense}}$$

Or

$$\text{DFL} = \frac{PQ - QV - F}{PQ - VQ - F - I}$$

$$\text{DFL} = \frac{Q(P-V) - F}{Q(P-V) - F - I}$$

In order to calculate DFL per share we can use earning per share instead of net income.

Interpretation: Let's say we have 1.5% DFL. It means if there is a change of 1% in EBIT, then the net income will change by 1.5%.

Degree of total leverage (DTL): Degree of total leverage is the combination of DOL and DFL.

DTL = DOL x DFL

$$\text{DTL} = \frac{\%\Delta\ EBIT}{\%\ \Delta\ in\ sales} \times \frac{\%\Delta\ net\ income}{\%\ \Delta\ EBIT}$$

Or

$$\text{DTL} = \frac{\%\Delta\ Net\ income}{\%\ \Delta\ in\ sales}$$

Or

$$\text{DTL} = \frac{Q(P-V)}{Q(P-V) - F - I}$$

It measures the sensitivity of net income towards sales. It measures the percentage changes in net income due to percentage change in sales.

Effect of financial leverage on a company's net income and return on equity

Return on equity (ROE) = Net income / Shares holders` equity

When we have some assets financed by debt capital, is will reduce the net income by interest paid. But when we calculate the ROE, we do not include debt in divider. So we come up with higher ROE. So in case of profit, ROE is magnified while in case of losses the ROE also magnifies the losses. The use of financial leverage also hits the net income in same way.

Breakeven quantity of sales and company's net income at various sales levels

Breakeven: Situation of no profit no loss is called breakeven. The quantity at which there is no profit and no loss is called breakeven quantity. (Total revenues = total cost). Any firm producing at less than breakeven point is facing loss. While, production after breakeven point is profitable.

Calculation of break-even quantity:
Breakeven is a point where

Total revenues = total cost
TR= TC
As
TR=price per unit x Quantity sold
TC = Variable cost + Fixed operating and fixed financial cost
so

PQ = Total Variable cost + Fixed operating cost + Fixed financing cost

PQ = QV + F + I

Solve for Q

PQ − QV = F + I

Q(P−v) = F+I

$$Q = \frac{(F+I)}{P-v}$$

We can use Q as Q_BE for break even quantity

$$Q_{BE} = \frac{(F+I)}{P-v}$$

F is the total fixed operating cost

I is the total financing cost

P is the per unit price

V is the per unit variable cost

With the help of this equation we can find our breakeven level of sales, given the fixed operating, financing and variable costs.

A positive "P-V" is the contribution margin per unit because it helps to cover fixed cost.

The breakeven point and net income at various sale levels can be expressed in graph.

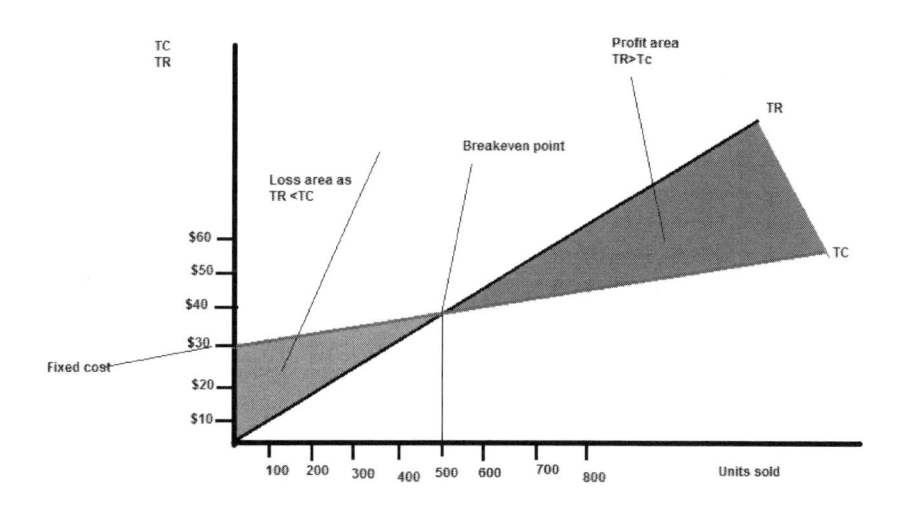

If the company sold units less than 500, it is bearing net loss. At 500 units it has no profit, no loss situation. After 500 units the firm will be in net profit. Farther the firm is from breakeven point more the firm will earn profits as the gap between TR and TC is increasing at every net unit of sale (in our case).

Operating breakeven quantity of sales

Operating breakeven point is same as we have discussed in previous section except here we only consider operating cost (ignore financing cost).

Q$_{OBE}$ = Operating fixed cost / (per unit price – per unit variable cost)

$$Q_{OBE} = \frac{F}{P - v}$$

So operating breakeven point means "the level of sales at which the total revenues are just equal to operating cost".

WORKING CAPITAL MANAGEMENT

Resources of liquidity

Companies need cash to meet short term obligations. The ability to generate cash at time of need with minimum or no cost is called liquidity.

There are two broad types of liquidity resources however they can vary from company to company; primary sources and secondary sources.

Primary sources: Use of primary sources of liquidity does not affect company`s normal course of business. The major primary sources of liquidity can include

- Balance in bank

- Cash received from customers
- Line of credit from bank
- Line of credit from company suppliers
- Account receivables
- Selling of short term investments
- Effective cash flow management

Secondary sources: The use of secondary sources of liquidity changes the normal course of business. It can change the capital structure of the company and its operations. Use of secondary sources can be a sign of poor management. Secondary sources of liquidity may include

- Negotiated or re-negotiated debt
- Selling current (inventory) and long lived assets
- Filing bankruptcy

Factors affecting liquidity position

Generally, early cash ins and slow cash outs are considered a good sign of cash management but it can vary from company to company and industry to industry. Usually the cash flow must match the industry traditions.

Broadly speaking there are two factors which weak the liquidity position of a company; the drags on liquidity and pulls on liquidity.

Drags on liquidity: Any factor which reduces the inflows of cash comes under this heading. Uncollected receivables, increase in bad debts, higher discounts on sales, inventory is getting obsolete (because it takes more time to sale) and higher cost of borrowings (tight credit) are "drags on liquidity".

Pulls on liquidity: All factors which pull out the cash from the company are pulls on liquidity. These factors are
Early payment
Reducing and or limiting the credit lines

Liquidity measures

A firm`s liquidity is measured with the help of liquidity ratios.

Liquidity ratios

Liquidity ratios measure a company's ability to meet its short-term obligations.

We have 3 major liquidity ratios, the current ratio, the quick ratio and the cash ratio.

Current ratio= Current assets /current liabilities.

Quick ratio= Liquid assets / current liabilities. Where, Liquid assets = cash+ marketable sec. + receivables

Cash ratio = (cash + marketable securities) / current liabilities.

Interpretations

A current ratio of one indicates that the company's current assets are equals the dollar value of their current liabilities. So, the short-term obligations are just covered. A ratio less than one means that the company is relying on operating profit to meet short term obligations because current assets are not enough.

Same interpretation is for following ratios too.

Quick ratio is more realistic approach about our ability to convert certain current assets into cash. Pre-payments for example might be included in the current assets of a company but would be are very difficult to turn into cash. Same is the case with inventory. So, we exclude these two in quick ratio to have more meaningful results.

With cash ratio we are more conservative about the asset`s ability to meet short-term obligations. We only include most liquid assets. We only include cash and marketable securities the company has right now to pay their short term obligations.

Inventory turnover ratio = Cost of goods sold / average inventory

It measures firm's efficiency in inventory management and its processing. It tells how many times the firm has sold its inventory completely (theoretically).

Number of days of inventory: It tells us the average processing period of inventory to turn into sales. It indicates on average how many days the firm takes to convert its inventory into sales.

Number of days of inventory = $\dfrac{Inventory}{COGS/365}$ = $\dfrac{Inventory}{COGS}$ x 365

Or

Number of days of inventory = $\dfrac{365}{Inventory\ turnover\ ratio}$

Payable turnover ratio = purchases/ average payables: It means how many times company pays its payables completely (theoretically).

Number of days of payables= 365/ payable turnover ratio: It tells us how many days a firm takes to pay its creditors.

These two should be close to industry norms. A relatively higher payables turnover (which would mean a relatively lower number of days payables are outstanding) the company might not be effectively taking advantage of credit facilities made available to them or they might be taking advantage of early payment discounts. We must look at the liquidity ratios to get proper understanding. If company has better liquidity ratios but higher days payable (lower payable turnover) it means they are taking advantage of available credit facilities. If liquidity position is bad with lower payable turnover they might be having trouble with cash generation.

Receivable turnover ratio= credit sales/ average receivables: It measures how many times the firm collects from its account receivables in a year. It measures the receivable liquidity management.

Number of days of receivables=Accounts receivable /average credit sales: It tells us on average how many days the firm takes to convert its receivables into cash.

Or

$$= \frac{Accounts\ receivable}{credit\ sales/365}$$

Or

$$= \frac{365}{Receivable\ turnover\ ratio}$$

How many days the firm takes to converts its account receivables into cash.

All these ratios must be analyzed carefully. As a general rule, the ratios must be close to industry average or to peer group.

Operating and cash conversion cycles

Operating cycle: It is the time period from the purchase of goods or materials through the sale of the product and the collection of cash.

Operating cycle = Days inventory in hand + Number of days of receivables

Cash conversion cycle (or Net Operating cycle) = {(days sales outstanding) + days inventory in hand) − (Number of days of payables)}

It is the time company takes to turn a product into cash (from cash paid to purchase inventory to receivable to cash collection).

A shorter Cash conversion cycle and Operating cycle means greater liquidity. It should be compared with industry norms. A longer of these two means too much investment is tied up into working capital.

Types of cash flows affect and net daily cash position

A firm can have several cash inflows and outflows during any given day. The net daily cash position is the net of these inflows and out flows. If the company has more inflows and less out flows it means firm has positive net cash position at the end of the day. These cash inflows and out flows should be managed by treasury department to make sure the firm has sufficient cash in hand at time of payment. The cash management department also has to ensure that they should not have more cash in hand than required. The extra cash should be invested in short term securities.

Typical routine cash inflows can be:

- Cash received from sales
- Cash received from receivables
- Cash received from subsidiaries
- Cash received from investments
- Tax refunds
- Borrowings
- Interest income etc

Typical outflows can be:

- Payment to suppliers
- Payment to payables
- Salaries
- Interest paid
- Tax payment
- Dividend payment
- Transfers to subsidiaries

Yields on various securities

Companies always try to invest the excessive cash which they need after a short time, to earn some return. Companies invest this excessive cash in short term securities with little or no risk. They can invest in

- T-bills
- Government securities
- Repurchase agreements
- Commercial papers
- Bank`s deposit certificates etc.

Yield on short term investment: The yield in any investment is the return an investor will earn by holding the investment until maturity. The major yield returns are as follows;

$$\text{Money market yield} = \frac{FV - \text{Purchase price}}{\text{Purchase price}} \times \frac{360}{\text{Number of days remaining to maturity}}$$

One thing to note here the money market yield considers 360 days in a year.

$$\text{Bond equivalent yield} = \frac{FV - \text{Purchase price}}{\text{Purchase price}} \times \frac{365}{\text{Number of days remaining to maturity}}$$

The bond equivalent yield considers 365 days in a year

$$\text{Discount basis yield} = \frac{FV - \text{Purchase price}}{FV} \times \frac{360}{\text{Number of days remaining to maturity}}$$

Discount basis yield is based on face value (FV) and considers 360 days in a year while the other two yields are based on purchase price.

Comparison against a benchmark: The performance of these short term investments must be compared with an appropriate benchmark. The benchmark could be an index or a security with same maturity and risk.

The returns on these investments should be consistent with their risk characteristics. Usually the companies are not looking for high risk and returns on these investments. The only purpose of these investments could be use of excessive cash to generate some return. There must be an investment policy for these investments which should be followed and properly monitored and evaluated from time to time. If the investment does not generate required returns the policy should be revised and again monitored and evaluated.

Management of accounts receivable, inventory, and accounts payable

The account receivables, payables and inventory must be managed effectively. If a company has large sales but is unable to cash its receivables, the company will face lack of liquidity. If the payables are not well managed, the relationships with suppliers will be deteriorated. If the inventory is piled up, a lot of working capital will be tied up there. Therefore, all these items contribute to the liquidity of the firm.

Account receivable management: Account receivable management means monitoring how quickly a firm cash out its account receivables. Two popular methods measures how well account receivables are managed; Account receivable aging schedule and number of days of account receivables.

Account receivable aging schedule: It is the weighted average collection days of receivables.

For example we make a schedule of what percentage of total receivables are cashed out in 30 days, 60 days and 90 days. This schedule can be maintained horizontally and can be compared with previous periods.

Number of days of account receivables:

Number of days of receivables=Accounts receivable /average credit sales: It tells us on average how many days the firm takes to convert its receivables into cash.

Or

Number of days of receivables = $\dfrac{Accounts\ receivable}{credit\ sales/365}$

This ratio can also be maintained horizontally and the company's account receivables can be compared with its previous periods management and also with peer group.

Inventory management:

Inventory turnover ratio= Cost of goods sold/ average inventory

It measures firm's efficiency in inventory management and its processing. It tells how many times the firm has sold its inventory completely (theoretically).

Number of days of inventory: It tells us the average processing period of inventory to turn into sales. It indicates on average how many days the firm takes to convert its inventory into sales.

Number of days of inventory = $\dfrac{Inventory}{COGS/365}$ = $\dfrac{Inventory}{COGS}$ x 365

Or

Number of days of inventory = $\dfrac{365}{Inventory\ turnover\ ratio}$

Account payable management:

Payable turnover ratio = purchases/ average payables: It means how many times company pays its payables completely (theoretically).

Number of days of payables= 365/ payable turnover ratio: It tells us how many days a firm takes to pay its creditors.

These two should be close to industry norms. A relatively higher payables turnover (which would mean a relatively lower number of days payables are outstanding) the company might not be effectively taking advantage of credit facilities made available to them or they might be taking advantage of early payment discounts. We must look at the liquidity ratios to get proper understanding. If company has better liquidity ratios but higher days payable (lower payable turnover) it means they are taking advantage of available credit facilities. If liquidity position is bad with lower payable turnover they might be having trouble with cash generation.

Choices of short-term funding

A firm can have several choices for short term funding. Examination of these choices is helpful for the analysts to understand if the company can fulfill its short term liquidity needs. We can divide short term funding into; Banking and non-banking funding choices.

Short term banking funding choices:

Uncommitted line of credit: The bank offers a certain amount but can effuse if the situation changes as there is no formal commitment from bank.

Committed or regular line of credit (Overdraft): It is a formal commitment from banks to extend loans (also called overdraft). The banks usually charge fee for such commitment.

Revolving credit line: This the strongest form of short term line of credit.

Collateral loan:

Discounted receivables: The firm sells it's receivable to a third party on discount (also called factoring).

Banker's acceptance: Usually involves in import and exports. The importer`s bank issue a certificate to exporter to ensure the timely payment after delivery.

Non-banking choices

Commercial papers
Non-bank credit institutes

Recommended financing method: The recommended financing choice is the one which is least costly for the firm. The firm must adopt that method which gives more proceeds per cost of borrowing.

$$Cost = \frac{Interest + processing\ fee + commission + any\ other\ fee}{Net\ proceeds\ for\ loan}$$

The method with least cost is preferred.

That's all for the Corporate Finance for CFA level 1. Hope you have enjoyed the book. Let me know if you have any question.

Ch.imranahsen@gmail.com
Whats app# 00923465006818

Printed in Great Britain
by Amazon